DANCERS OF TO-DAY NO. 11

NADIA NERINA

Taking a call

An action photograph by G. B. L. Wilson

IN *BIRTHDAY OFFERING*

Photograph by Houston Rogers

NADIA NERINA

by

CYRIL SWINSON

LONDON
ADAM AND CHARLES BLACK

FIRST PUBLISHED 1957

4, 5 & 6 SOHO SQUARE
LONDON, W.1

A recent photograph by Houston Rogers

AUTHOR'S NOTE

I am most grateful to Miss Elsa Brunelleschi, Mr. Claude Newman and Mr. Michael Wood for their help during the preparation of this book. I am grateful also to Mr. G. B. L. Wilson for allowing me to use a number of his photographs, some of which are now published for the first time, to Mr. Ian Purvis and Miss Elise Baxter for their help in collecting many of the photographs used in this book, and to Mr. Arthur H. Franks and Miss Mary Clarke of *The Dancing Times*, for allowing me to use several photographs from their collection.

C. S.

CONTENTS

MADE IN GREAT BRITAIN
PRINTED BY MORRISON AND GIBB LIMITED, LONDON AND EDINBURGH

INTRODUCTION

WHEN Nadine Judd arrived in England for the first time on the 1st November 1945 she had never seen a performance by a professional ballet company. If one had been told then, that within six years she would have become a ballerina of the Sadler's Wells Ballet it would have seemed highly improbable. Nevertheless, she did in fact achieve this position in 1951 under the name of Nadia Nerina. To-day, Miss Nerina is a ballerina with an international reputation, in America, on the Continent and in South Africa. Her dancing has great verve and style; she has great confidence in all that she does and a crisp and assured technique. She has charm, good looks, great vitality and a natural gaiety.

A zest for work, intelligence and a determination to succeed have been integral parts of her personality from an early age. She was born in Cape Town, South Africa, in October 1927. When she was nine years old, and her family were living in Bloemfontein, she was sent to her first dancing classes, not because she had shown any exceptional aptitude for dancing but because it was the accepted thing for all young girls to do. Her father's business necessitated moving about the country and later the family moved to Durban. Here her parents found two excellent teachers, Eileen Keegan, who had been a pupil of Margaret Craske, and Dorothea McNair. It was soon evident to her teachers that the child possessed exceptional promise and Nadine Judd began to study dancing seriously, so seriously in fact that when her family later moved to Johannesburg, she persuaded her parents to allow her to return to Durban alone since there were at that time no suitable teachers available in Johannesburg.

Thus she had to develop at an early age her self-possession and self-confidence, and her mother's early death during this period increased still further the child's ability to stand on her own feet and strengthened her determination to devote her life to the career to which she seemed most fitted.

She had shown promise as an actress but ballet was her final choice. She realised, however, that if she was to make dancing her profession she must come to London for further training. At this time, immediately after the war, it was difficult to obtain a passage, but by persistent visits to every shipping agency she secured finally a berth on a Swedish cargo boat, which docked at Liverpool on 1st November 1945. When she reached London she telephoned Mme Marie Rambert, the only person whose name she knew, and secured permission to join her classes. Later she went to Miss Elsa Brunelleschi for special coaching, and subsequently appeared in two of Miss Brunelleschi's recitals. Miss Brunelleschi remembers her at that time: "She was perhaps over-supple and she needed to learn some restraint. There was no doubt at all about her potentiality: one would have to be blind not to have recognised it." It was not only her technical ability which impressed Miss Brunelleschi. "She had a great zest for work, a quiet determination and a most attractive and vivacious personality. On the stage of the small hall in which the recitals were given her performance had such vitality and force it filled the hall. I have never seen anything like it."

On 1st February 1946 she joined the Sadler's Wells School and a few weeks later, on 26th February, she took part in the first performance of *The Sleeping Beauty* with which the Royal Opera House in London was reopened. She was one of the nurses in attendance on the infant Aurora. Six years later she danced the part of Aurora herself on the same stage.

When she had been a pupil at the Sadler's Wells School for less than two months she was invited to join the Sadler's Wells Opera Ballet, which became the Sadler's Wells Theatre Ballet the following year. Nadia Nerina (as she had decided to call herself) was in the *corps de ballet* when the company gave its first performance of *Les Sylphides* on 22nd April 1946. "Nerina" was her mother's name and also the name of a South African lily. Later, for a short time, she called herself Nadia Moore, but soon reverted to the attractive name by which she is now known.

In the eighteen months that she was with the company she graduated from the *corps de ballet* to become a leading dancer. Claude Newman, who was ballet master for the company at that time, remembers her especially for her zeal for work and her untiring energy; at class and rehearsals she was the first to arrive and usually the last to leave, and Newman discovered that she had persuaded the caretaker to let her in an hour before class started so that she could practise on her own. Indeed, she worked so hard that she had to be persuaded to take things a little more easily, an attitude of mind she has always found it hard to accept. Her stamina and vitality are extraordinary: she never seems to tire, and in later years, after a strenuous performance of *Ballet Highlights*, when she and her partner Alexis Rassine have occupied the stage for the entire evening, her vitality seems undiminished. This vitality and the strength of her technique made her outstanding in a company of most-promising young dancers and it was not long before she was dancing the Sugar Plum Fairy in *Casse-Noisette* and other leading rôles (see pages 8–10).

On the 1st December 1947 Nadia Nerina joined the Sadler's Wells Ballet and two days later she was dancing the Mazurka in *Les Sylphides*, partnered by Alexis Rassine, who was to be her principal partner for several years. She made good progress in the company, acquiring a number of interesting rôles, including the Fairy Spring in Ashton's new full-length ballet *Cinderella*.

Early in 1951, on the first night of Ashton's *Daphnis and Chloe*, she appeared as Odette in Act II of *Le Lac des Cygnes*. It was a good performance technically, and held out great promise for the future. Later in 1951 she learned the rôle of Mam'zelle Angot in three days, and gave an assured performance in the part, bringing great vitality and gaiety to the rôle and making Mam'zelle Angot quite irresistible. As a result of this one felt that Miss Nerina was essentially a *soubrette* or a *demi-caractère* dancer, and this was confirmed by her performance in *Coppélia*, where she made Swanilda a gay and mischievous peasant girl, recalling the gaiety and precision of the young Danilova.

The absence of Fonteyn, Grey and Elvin at various times in 1953 and 1954 gave her exceptional opportunities to dance the major rôles in classical ballet. In dancing these she showed a quite remarkable restraint and gave a much more than technically competent interpretation. She was a great success in America, and John Martin, the distinguished critic of the *New York Times*, found her " completely adorable." " She is pretty as a picture," he said in his review of her Princess Aurora, " has great charm and can dance like a million dollars. Her body is beautifully placed, giving her lovely free arms and an unusually articulated torso. There are simply no problems of movement for her, and never so much as a hint of an ugly one. When Miss Nerina has developed a musical phrase to equal her command of the physical medium, we shall all be fighting to drink champagne out of her slippers."

Miss Nerina now dances all the major rôles in the classical ballet : Odette-Odile, Princess Aurora, Giselle and Swanilda, and the parts of Sylvia and Cinderella in Ashton's full-length ballets ; a record of achievement she was the first to share with the *prima ballerina assoluta*, Dame Margot Fonteyn.

In 1956 she made notable progress both in her classical rôles and in a new ballet, *Noctambules*, by Kenneth MacMillan, in which she created the leading rôle of the Faded Ballerina. She danced beautifully and made a great contribution to the success of this arresting and original work.

Later in the season she appeared with the other ballerinas of the company in Frederick Ashton's *pièce d'occasion*, *Birthday Offering*, which was created for the twenty-fifth birthday performance of the company. Her variation, with its electric jumps and *double tours en l'air*, was one of the sensations of the evening. She danced better than ever before in this season, and her lovely clean line and her immaculate finish made her a most exciting dancer to watch. The title rôle in *The Firebird*, the Doll in *Petrushka* and the Ballerina in *Ballet Imperial* are among her latest rôles.

The ultimate perfection of Odette-Odile and her other rôles in classical ballet, is still to be achieved, although often there are wonderful moments in her performances which make it safe to predict that her interpretations will continue to grow in feeling and emotional depth. It seems to me that technically she has little more to learn, and for her development as an artist, rather than as a virtuoso of the dance, she needs to be more relaxed and less intense. In character and personality Miss Nerina is an exceptional young woman and I believe that she is capable of a much deeper and more personal interpretation of the great ballerina rôles than she has so far achieved. She needs, perhaps, above all the guidance which can only be given to her by a teacher with great theatrical experience ; a teacher who will not impose her will on the pupil but one who will seek to increase her individuality and powers of expression.

Nadia Nerina is a dancer of great virtuosity, a joy to watch and a delight to the countless thousands of people who have seen her dance on television, on her recital tours in England and South Africa, and as a ballerina of The Royal Ballet. But the artist, and Miss Nerina is potentially a much greater artist than she is at present, does not want merely to be acclaimed for miracles of virtuosity. True satisfaction comes in other ways, and although perfection remains unattainable the true artist continues the journey. May all good fortune attend Miss Nerina's future : few artists can have worked harder or deserved more to achieve success.

In private life Miss Nerina is married to Mr. Charles Gordon, a fellow South African.

ıree early photographs by Studio ager, Johannesburg, 1943. *Right:* In Spanish dance. *Below, left:* In *The* *ker* by Eileen Keegan; *right:* In a ıssical solo

Mandinian

BAILEMOS: With Sheilah O'Reilly (1946)

Sharland

Columbine in *CARNAVAL* (1947)

MARDI GRAS: As the Circus Dancer, her first created rôle. With Donald Britton as the Boy (1946)

Mandinian

Keyst

SADLER'S WELLS THEATRE BALLET

LES SYLPHIDES

Photograph by Gordon Anthony

At the first performance of this ballet by the company, Nadia Nerina was in the *corps de ballet.* Later she danced the soloist rôles : the valse, the first mazurka, the prelude and the *pas de deux*

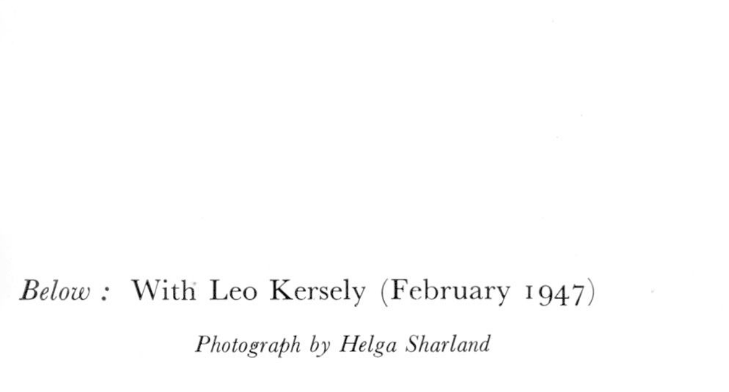

Below : With Leo Kersely (February 1947)

Photograph by Helga Sharland

SADLER'S WELLS BALLET

Nadia Nerina joined the Sadler's Wells Ballet on 1st December 1947.

Helga Sharland

In her costume for the *pas de trois* in *SWAN LAKE* (March 1948)

Helga Sharl

In *BOUTIQUE FANTASQUE*, the Can Can Dancer (September 1948)

Photograph by Roger Wood

CINDERELLA : The Fairy Spring. This rôle, in Ashton's first full-length ballet, was her first creation for the Sadler's Wells Ballet (23rd December 1948)

Rehearsing with Alexander Grant on the company's first American tour (1949)

Photograph by Walter E. Owen

Below, left : The Tango from *FAÇADE*, with Alexander Grant (1950)

Maurice Seymour

Below, right : The Polka from *FAÇADE*

Edward Mandinian

Opposite : The Bride in *A WEDDING BOUQUET*

Maurice Seymour

CINDERELLA

Nadia Nerina danced the title rôle for the first time at the Royal Opera House, Covent Garden, on 16th February 1951

Above : In Act I
Gordon Anthony

Below, left : At the Ball
Gordon Anthony

Below, right : Curtain call, with Ashton, Robert Irving and Alexis Rassine
G. B. L. Wilson

Right : With Desmond Doyle as the Prince.
John Baker

THE SLEEPING BEAUTY

Nadia Nerina made her first appearance as Aurora on 12th January 1952. (She was a nursemaid in the Prologue at the re-opening of the Royal Opera House on 20th February 1946, and after she had joined the Company in 1947 she had danced the Fairy of the Woodland Glades, in the Florestan *pas de trois*, and in the Bluebird *pas de deux.*)

Above : In Act I

An action photograph by G. B. L. Wilson

Right : With Alexis Rassine

Houston Rogers

Opposite : In the Rose Adagio

Houston Rogers

SWAN LAKE

Right : With Alexis Rassine

Photographs by Maurice Seymour

Nadia Nerina first danced Odette in the second act of the ballet with the Sadler's Wells Theatre Ballet. Her début in the part at Covent Garden was on 5th April 1951. She danced the dual rôle of Odette-Odile for the first time on 20th December 1952

Angus McBean

SYLVIA: First performance in the title rôle (26th November 1952)

COPPÉLIA, Act I : Swanilda and her friends

COPPÉLIA

New production, revised by Ninette de Valois, with scenery and costumes by Osbert Lancaster, first performed at Covent Garden, 2nd March 1954

Act II : In Dr. Coppelius's workshop. With Frederick Ashton as Dr. Coppelius

With David Blair. Nadia Nerina had danced Swanilda many times in an earlier production, and in the new version she was partnered on the first night by David Blair

Photographs page 20 : Houston Rogers (top), Topical Press (bottom) and (centre) page 21. Above : Denis de Marney ; below : G. B. L. Wilson

Curtain call with Blair, de Valois and Ashton

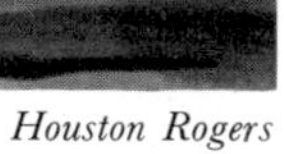

Houston Rogers

GISELLE

Nadia Nerina first danced Giselle in South Africa in 1955 ; her first performance in London was at the Royal Opera House, Covent Garden, 7th April 1956

Above : In Act I

Above right : The end of Act I

Below right : In Act II

Edwin Smit

Houston Rogers

SCÈNES DE BALLET: In the ballerina rôle

Above, left : In *HOMAGE TO THE QUEEN*, the Queen of the Earth, with Alexis Rassine (2nd June 1953). *Above, right : VARIATIONS ON A THEME OF PURCELL*, one of the three ballerinas (6th January 1955). *Above : PETRUSHKA*, The Doll (30th March 1957)

All photographs by Houston Rogers

Houston Rogers

BALLET IMPERIAL: Revived in 1957. Nadia Nerina, partnered by Philip Chatfield, danced the Golden Ballerina

Houston Rog

THE FIREBIRD: Nadia Nerina first danced the Firebird in London, 24th September 1956, with Michael Somes as Ivan Tsarevitch

NOCTAMBULES

First performance 1st March 1956
Music : Humphrey Searle

Scenario and choreography : Kenneth MacMillan

Costumes and scenery : Nicholas Georgiadis

In this, her first major creation, Nadia Nerina danced the part of the Faded Ballerina, who, under the influence of the Hypnotist (Leslie Edwards) regains her youth and beauty

Serge Lido

Above : With Leslie Edwards

Three action photographs by G. B. L. Wilson showing Nerina in her spectacular solo and in her dance with the Hypnotist and four young men

G. B. L. Wilson

BALLET HIGHLIGHTS

and other solos and dances

Above : Taking a call
Below : In *The Dying Swan*

Houston Rogers

MORE BALLET HIGHLIGHTS

Left : In *THE DRAGONFLY*, a solo created and danced by Pavlova

Below, left : In the *DON QUIXOTE pas de deux*

A photograph taken at the Pavlova Gala 1956 by Paul Wilson

Below, right : FIREBIRD pas de deux specially created in 1956 by Kenneth MacMillan for Nadia Nerina and Alexis Rassine

Photograph by permission of George Outram & Co. Ltd

Jane Plotz

Mike Dav

BALLET HIGHLIGHTS

(*Continued*)

Above: SPECTRE DE LA ROSE, with Alexis Rassine

Above, right: In her *Don Quixote* costume

Right: L'APRÈS MIDI D'UN FAUNE, with Alexis Rassine

Houston Rogers

Houston Rogers

BOLERAS DE LA CACHUCHA: A *pas de deux* specially created by Elsa Brunelleschi for Nadia Nerina and Alexis Rassine

1946 : With Anne Heaton (left) and (centre)
Sheilah O'Reilly

1947 : On tour. David Poole, Jane Shore
Nadia Nerina, Elaine Fifield

1948

1950 : *En route* for the U.S.A.

1951 : At Cambridge

1956 : With Walford Hyden (*left*) and Phili
J. S. Richardson

FROM G. B. L. WILSON'S SCRAPBOOK

The photographs are all by G. B. L. Wilson, excepting bottom right, which is by Paul Wilson